Foundations

8-week Bible Course

Identity

Eternal Life

The Goal

How to Read your Bible

Baptisms

The New Covenant

Entering God`s Rest

Church

COPYRIGHT

DEDICATION

TO MY GOD AND FAMILY for all the love, faith, grace, and light.

ENDORSEMENTS

———

"**F**oundations 8-week Bible Course is instructive, effective, practical, and easy to understand. It accurately reflects the power and grace of the Word to change lives. A rare find amongst many alternative Christian Study guides that are available. I`m sure that those making use of the course, by applying the biblical truths therein, will bear much fruit in the Kingdom."

~Craig Fyall, Lead Pastor Jesus Factor, Brazil

"This is probably the best foundational manual I have come across. I am planning to teach it at church as it literally has everything, I would want a believer to know "crammed" in a few Pages but worthy to be studied line by line."

~Humbulani Nemakonde, Lead Pastor Grace, South Africa

"Paul does an excellent job explaining fundamental grace to new believers. With so much law, religion, and legalistic striving in the Christian world, it is more important than ever to establish structures of discipleship that bring transformative grace and truth of the new covenant. New and seasoned believers will benefit greatly from this course book."

~Cedric Van Duyn, Lead Pastor Anthem Church, WA USA

FOREWORD

"Foundations" ... is a powerful grace-based church resource that will set up believers, new and old to live in the power of the finished work of Christ as victorious overcoming believers.

Any church leader who's looking to resource their team to equip the saints in building a strong Gospel centered biblical foundation would find "Foundations" to be a practical tool and timeless resource.

~James Monaghan

INTRODUCTION
Why it's Vital

<hr>

As with many in the Church I have done a full circle of sorts. Being born into Catholicism, and later in my early twenties attending the Pentecostal Church. With a detour later into Seven-day Adventism in my late twenties and finally where for the last 20 plus years growing in my understanding of my sonship to all Christ has accomplished on the Cross in several non-denominational churches.

This course is the essentials I pray I knew at the very beginning of my walk in and with Christ. It would have saved me a lot of anxiety, anguish, and time. I have taught many, 4-week, 8-week, 12-week, and one-year foundational, discipleship or discovery courses over the years. And the usual questions arise. Sometimes in large groups of over a hundred to smaller groups of 4. This is by no means a hard to read or very in-depth course. Rather it is for the beginner, or anyone wanting to relay those foundation stones firmly within their souls and renew their minds to the gospel truth. The eternal and fantastic news of the too good to be true good news of Jesus. Love you all and pray the leading of the Holy Spirit enlightens His truth not only into your mind but your hearts too.

Now let's start week 1.

WEEK ONE
Identity

———

(WHO ARE YOU?)

It's our birth that dictates our family and inheritance. But our identity is what defines us. Our identity is often linked to what we do, what we like, where we're from, or how we see ourselves. Have you ever noticed how people introduce themselves for the first time?

"Good morning. My name's Mr. Smith. I'm an electrician."

"Hi, I'm Allen. I teach 7th grade history."

"Hello everyone. My name is John. I'm an alcoholic." Our identity defines us.

Prior to us accepting Christ's life and His saving grace, what we did defined us. Adam defined us. In Romans 3:23 Paul the Apostle tells us that, "All have sinned and fall short of the glory of God." (The Fathers perfected manifested character: Jesus). It doesn't matter if we've sinned a little or a lot, everyone has sinned, and a sinner was who we identified as. You see it took zero sins to be a sinner you only had to have been born. For we were all born in Adams sin.

So unfair you might be thinking, but how Good is it that Jesus offers His free gift of salvation. (HEALS, RESTORES, SAVES, PROTECTS, BLESSES, and MAKES WHOLE) to all.

No conditions apply. Believe it by faith. Receive it by faith. Being a sinner was who we were before Christ. We could not help ourselves.

But when you heard the good news of Jesus You repented. You thought differently and changed direction. That you are a sinner and in need of a saviour from sin by placing faith in Christ. Receiving His free gift of righteousness (right standing). And at that moment you received a brand-new spirit, heart, nature, and identity.

"If anyone is in Christ, he is a new creation" (2 Cor 5:17). I'm sure many of us have quoted this verse many times but have you thought about what it means to be new? To be Made NEW: this is to say <u>You are not improved, re-modified, re-tweaked, re-conditioned, re-upholstered, re-vamped or re-branded.</u> **You are wholly new**. A never-before-seen creation. A one of a kind. Indeed, a new creature. Something that you never were before not something re-modelled.

This identity took place in your new created **BORN-AGAIN SPIRIT.** This means that if you had red hair before you got born again you had red hair after you were born again. The change was internal at your very core.

A new core has now replaced the old. You <u>are no longer defined by your sin; Christ's righteousness now defines you.</u>

Paul the Apostle said, "I have been crucified with Christ; and it is no longer I who live, but Christ lives in me" (Galatians 2:20). Christ lives in you and wants to live His very life through You.

Before we go on, have you made the decision to receive Jesus`s Life (born again)?

God's Word promises, "If thou shalt confess with thy mouth the Lord Jesus, and shalt believe in thine heart that God hath raised him from the dead, thou shalt be saved. For with the heart man believeth unto righteousness; and with the mouth confession is made unto salvation.... For whosoever shall call upon the name of the Lord shall be saved" (Rom. 10:9–10,13).

By His grace, God has already done everything to provide salvation. Your part is to believe and receive it.

Let's all Pray out loud,

Jesus, I confess that You are my Lord and Saviour. I believe in my heart that God raised You from the dead, that you paid all my sin debt and offer me your very own life. By faith in Your, I receive eternal salvation now. Thank You for saving me. You are my God and saviour!

Romans 6:6-8 We know that our old (unrenewed) self was nailed to the cross with Him in order that [our] body [which is the instrument] of sin might be made ineffective and inactive for evil, that we might no longer be the slaves of sin. 7 For when a man dies, he is freed (loosed, delivered) from [the power of] sin [among men].

8 Now if we have died with Christ, we believe that we shall also live with Him, (side note sin here is singular and a noun, meaning a place, thing, or person).

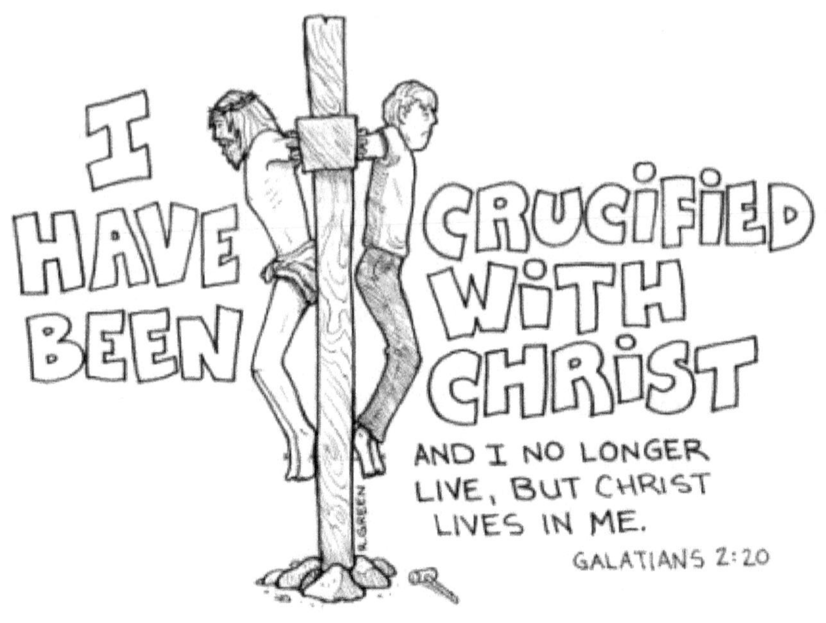

THE BEAUTIFUL EXCHANGE that took place on the cross (Christ saving you and giving you His identity) restoring that which had was lost. Let's read Romans 6:6-8 through the lens of the Cross.

"Who died on the cross? Of course, our blessed Lord died on the cross, but who else died there? Knowing this, that our old self was crucified with him, in order that our body of sin might be done away with, so that we would no longer be slaves to sin; for he who has died is freed from sin. Now if we have died with Christ, we believe that we shall also live with Him.'"

As a Christian, your new identity is found in Christ. When He died on the cross, you died on the cross (Romans 6:6–8).

When He rose from the dead, you rose from the dead (Colossians 2:12 having been buried with Him in baptism, in which you were also raised up with Him through faith in the working of God, who raised Him from the dead.). You are in Christ and Christ is in you. He is your identity. You are now a carrier of His very own divine nature. The same very nature as Jesus. This is what water baptism represents. An inward change expressed outwardly by faith.

It simply means that your old You has passed away, and your new life is found in Christ (2 Corinthians 5:17 Therefore if anyone is in Christ, [a]he is a new creature; the old things passed away; behold, new things have come).

Now this does not mean that you will never sin again or that the residue effects from the old you will try reminding you of the old you. That is simply the flesh (the old way of thinking-the carnal mind)!

Now that you're new, do you know who you are?

<u>Below is a list of things you need to know about your new God-given identity</u>. Let us read these words out loud, with conviction, and I guarantee you it will leave you feeling mightily encouraged... and new.

I am a saint, a trophy of Christ's victory

I am born again of imperishable seed

I am a new creation, complete in Christ and perfect forever

I am a child of God, the apple of my Father's eye

I am one with the Lord and the temple of the Holy Spirit

I am eternally redeemed and completely forgiven

I am seated with Christ in heavenly realms

I am summoned by name, and I am His

I am dead to sin and alive to God

I am free from guilt and condemnation

I am righteous, holy, and blameless!

I am healed and I am strong in the Lord

I am hidden in Christ and eternally secure

I am loved with an everlasting love, and I am highly favoured

I am my Beloved's, and He is mine

I am the head and not the tail

I am blessed with every spiritual blessing, and I am a joint heir with Christ

I am a competent minister of the new covenant

I am bona fide and qualified, chosen and anointed

I am His royal ambassador, a missionary to the world

I am a stranger on earth, a citizen of a city whose maker is God

I am not looking back but I am pressing on to know Him more

I am trusting that He will finish in me that which He started

I am a king and a priest, a carrier of the Lord's authority

I am a healer of the sick and a demon's worst nightmare

I am king o' the world because His victory is mine!

I am as bold as a lion and more than a conqueror

I am a towering testimony of the Spirit's power

I am the salt of the earth and the light of the world

I am the sweet smell of Jesus to those who are perishing

I am a tree planted by the water, and I am a fruitful branch

I am the disciple whom Jesus loves

And by the grace of God, I am what I am!!!

Sources:

I am a saint (Rm 1:7, Eph 1:1, Php 1:1 Ju 1:3), a trophy of Christ's victory (2 Cor 2:14, AMP); born again (1 Pe 1:23), a new creation (2 Cor 5:17); complete in Christ (Col 2:10) and perfect forever (He 10:14); a child of God (1 Jn 3:1), the apple of my Father's eye (Ps 17:8); one with the Lord (1 Cor 6:17) and the temple of the Holy Spirit (1 Cor 6:19); eternally redeemed (He 9:12) and completely forgiven (Col 2:13); seated with Christ in heavenly realms (Eph 2:6); summoned by name and His (Is 43:1, 2 Cor 1:22); dead to sin and alive to God (Rm 6:11); free from guilt and condemnation (He 10:22, Rm 8:1); righteous (2 Cor 5:21), holy and blameless! (Eph 1:4); healed (1 Pet 2:24) and strong in the Lord (Eph 6:10); hidden in Christ (Col 3:3) and eternally secure (He 6:19); loved with an everlasting love (Jer 31:3); highly favored (Eph 1:6 charitoo); my Beloved's and He is mine (Son 6:3); the head and not the tail (De 28:13); blessed with every spiritual blessing (Eph 1:3) and a joint heir with Christ (Rm 8:17); a competent minister of the new covenant (2 Co 3:6); bona fide and qualified (Col 1:12), chosen (Jn 15:8, Col 3:12, 1 Th 1:4, 1 Pe 2:9) and anointed (1 Jn 2:27); His royal ambassador (2 Co 5:20), a missionary to the world (Mt 28:19); a stranger on earth (He 11:13), a citizen of a city whose maker is God (He 11:10,16, 12:22); pressing on to know Him more (Ph 3:14); He will finish what He started (He 12:2, Ju 1:24, 2 Co 9:8); a king and a priest (Rev 1:6); a carrier of the Lord's authority (Lk 10:19); a healer of the sick (Mark 16:18) and a demon's worst nightmare (Mt 10:8); king o' the world (1 Jn 5:4) because

His victory is mine (1 Co 15:57); as bold as a lion (Pr 28:1) and more than a conqueror (Rm 8:37);

a testimony of the Spirit's power (1 Cor 2:4, 12:7, 2 Co 1:9); the salt (Mt 5:13) and light of the world (Mt 5:14); the sweet smell of Jesus to those who are perishing (2 Cor 2:15); a tree planted by the water (Ps 1:3, Jer 17:7), and a fruitful branch (Jn 15:8); the disciple whom Jesus loves (Eph 1:6) and by the grace of God I am what I am (1 Co 15:10). You are the salt of the earth (Matt. 5:13) You are the light of the world (Matt. 5:14) You are a child of God (part of His family) (Jn. 1:12; Rom. 8:16) You are part of the true vine (Jn. 15:1, 5) You are Christ's friend (Jn. 15:15) You are chosen and appointed by Christ to bear His fruit (Jn. 15:16) You are a personal witness of Christ (Acts 1:8) You are a slave of righteousness. (Rom. 6:18) You are enslaved to God (Rom. 6:22) You are a child of God (Rom. 8:14, 15; Gal. 3:26; 4:6) You are a joint-heir with Christ (Rom. 8:17) You are a temple of God (1 Cor. 3:16; 6:19) You are joined to the Lord and are one spirit with Him (1 Cor. 6:17) You are a member of Christ's body (1 Cor. 12:27; Eph. 5:30) You are a new creation (2 Cor. 5:17) You are reconciled to God and a minister of reconciliation (2 Cor. 5:18–19) You are a son of God and one in Christ (Gal.3:26–28) You are an heir of God (Gal. 4:6–7) You are a saint (Eph. 1:1; 1 Cor. 1:2; Phil. 1:1, Col. 1:2) You are God's workmanship (Eph. 2:10) You are a fellow citizen in His family (Eph. 2:19) You are a prisoner of Christ (Eph. 3:1; 4:1) You are righteous and holy (Eph. 4:24) You are a citizen of heaven and seated in heaven right now (Phil. 3:20; Eph. 2:6) You are hidden with Christ in God (Col. 3:3) You are an expression of the life of Christ (Col. 3:4) You are chosen of God, holy, and dearly loved (Col. 3:12) You are chosen and dearly loved by God (1 Thess. 1:4) You are a son of light and not of darkness (1 Thess. 5:5) You are a holy brother, partaker of a heavenly calling (Heb. 3:1) You are a partaker of Christ (Heb. 3:14) You are a living stone (1 Pet. 2:5) You are a chosen race, a royal priesthood, a holy nation (1 Pet. 2:9–10) You are an alien and stranger to this world (1 Pet. 2:11) You are an enemy of the devil (1

Pet. 5:8) You are a child of God (1 Jn. 3:1–2) You are born of God and the evil one (the devil) can't touch you (1 Jn. 5:18) You are a sheep of His pasture (Ps. 23 and 100.)

A major part of Christian living is beginning to see yourself from God's perspective: Just as JESUS IS!!! Take the time to highlight the ones that mean the most to you. A great way is to stand in front of a mirror seeing yourself and saying what the Father says about You. Apply this to daily your living, over yourself, family etc

NOTES

WEEK TWO
Eternal Life

A REMARKABLY FAMILIAR scripture most of us have heard is John 3:16 which says, "For God so loved the world that he gave his only begotten Son, that whosoever believeth in him should not perish but have <u>everlasting life</u>."

This scripture has been used to teach that Jesus came and died for our sins so that we wouldn't perish. As true as this is, this verse is saying much more. Jesus coming and dying for us was so that we could have everlasting life. It just so happened we were dead in our sin which was a barrier that stood between us and this everlasting life. There is so much more to the Cross than just Jesus dying for our sins. Part of the Gospel is not that Jesus came to make bad men (mankind) good. But to make dead men (mankind) alive. There is so much more to the Gospel. There is so much more to Jesus!

Jesus spoke regularly about eternal life. He said...

"Whoever believes in Him will have eternal life." John 3:15

"For this is the will of My Father, that everyone who beholds the Son and believes in Him will have eternal life..." John 6:40

"For God so loved the world, that He gave His only begotten Son, that whoever believes in Him shall not perish, but have eternal life." John 3:16

"...the water that I will give him will become...a well of water springing up to eternal life." John 4:14

The purpose of salvation is not living forever in heaven one day, as awesome as that will be.

Based on Scripture, we know that those who believe in Christ will have eternal life. But what is eternal life?

"This is eternal life, that they may know You, the only true God, and Jesus Christ whom You have sent" John 17:3

The real purpose of salvation is to have intimacy—a personal relationship with the Lord God. Part of Salvation in essence was to get Heaven into You. There are multitudes of people who have cried out to God for the forgiveness of their sins but have never had intimacy with God as their reason for being born again. Many simply saw it as a form of fire insurance. This is not to say they are not saved.

Eternal life is to know the Father. The reason Christ set aside the glory of heaven and came to earth is that we may know Him.

God's primary gift is Himself. He is the very source of LIFE. We were created for relationship with God, sin separated that relationship, and Jesus died and rose again to reconcile the relationship. Eternal life is to know God relationally. The Father has always been the initiator of relationship. Even in the Garden when Adam and Eve sinned and hide away, He sought them out.

In short, the root of eternal life is knowing Jesus, the fruit is life eternal!

If eternal life is to know God, how do we get to know Him?

First: God must reveal Himself.

Second: We must believe what He has revealed.

Third: We must spend time with the revealed One.

How has God revealed Himself? He has revealed Himself through...

• **Creation** (Psalm 19:1–4 [1]The heavens proclaim the glory of God. The skies display his craftsmanship [2]Day after day they continue to speak; night after night they make him known. [3]They speak without a sound or word; their voice is never heard. [4]Yet their message has gone throughout the earth, and their words to all the world. God has made a home in the heavens for the sun; Romans 1:20 For ever since the world was created, people have seen the earth and sky. Through everything God made, they can clearly see his invisible qualities—his eternal power and divine nature. So, they have no excuse for not knowing God.)

• **Conscience** (Romans 2:14–15 Even Gentiles, who do not have God's written law, show that they know his law when they instinctively obey it, even without having heard it.

15 They demonstrate that God's law is written in their hearts, for their own conscience and thoughts either accuse them or tell them they are doing right.)

• **Christ** (John 1:1 In the beginning the Word already existed. The Word was with God, and the Word was God, John 5:18 So the Jewish leaders tried all the harder to find a way to kill him. For he not only broke the Sabbath, he called God his Father, thereby making himself equal with God, John 8:58 Jesus said to them, `Verily, verily, I say to you, Before Abraham's coming—I am; John 14:9 Jesus said to him, "Have I been so long with you, and yet you have not come to know Me, Philip? He who has seen Me has seen the Father; how can you say, 'Show us the Father';

Hebrews 1:1–2 In many parts, and many ways, God of old having spoken to the fathers in the prophets, 2 in these last days did speak to us in a Son, whom He appointed heir of all things, through whom also He did make the ages;)

• **The Bible** (John 20:31 but these have been written so that you may believe that Jesus is the Christ, the Son of God; and that believing you may have life in His name.; 2 Timothy 3:16 All Scripture is [a]inspired by God and profitable for teaching, for reproof, for correction, for [b]training in righteousness; 2 Peter 1:21 for no prophecy was ever made by an act of human will, but men moved by the Holy Spirit spoke from God.)

<u>Why is it important to believe what God has revealed</u>? Faith is central to the Gospel message. As we saw through the Scriptures on the previous page, eternal life is given to those who believe in Christ. It is not Grace alone that saves, just as it is not faith alone that saves.

Ephesians 2:8-9 Paul the Apostle speaking gives us the bases for salvation. And it reads, "8God saved you by his grace when you believed (by faith). And you can't take credit for this; it is a gift from God. 9Salvation is not a reward for the good things we have done, so none of us can boast about it. As we have seen it is a combination of both. That means a person believes that Jesus is the Son of God and that He died on the cross, rose from the dead, and offers eternal life. Who Christ is and what Christ did on the cross is the core of the Gospel message. It must be believed by faith. His saving Grace is accessed by faith!

Finally, we must spend time with the object of our faith: Jesus. The only way to get to know someone is to spend time with that person. You can learn about someone from a book, but you get to know that person by spending time together. It is all about knowing Him. And We see the Fathers true nature and character when we look at Jesus. As you're with someone, you pick up their mannerisms, likes and dislikes, temperament, attitude, outlook, heart, there way of thinking, and how they respond. You get to know a person by spending time with that person. Jesus said all I do is what I see my father do.

(John 5:19 therefore Jesus answered and was saying to them, "Truly, truly, I say to you, the Son can do nothing of Himself, unless it is something He sees the Father doing; for whatever [a] the Father does, these things the Son also does in like manner.)

Knowing the Father.

God's gift is eternal life. Eternal life is to know God. We get to know God because He has revealed Himself, by believing what He has revealed, and by spending time with Him. Knowing Him, being in union and communion with the One who is eternal!

Look up John 15:1–8 in your Bible. How many times does Christ tell us to abide? To abide means to stay with Him, remain in Him, be at home in Him. Based on what you've read, how does abiding in Christ help you to know God?

John 15:1-8 "I am the true vine, and My Father is the vinedresser. 2 Every branch in Me that does not bear fruit, He takes away; and every branch that bears fruit, He prunes it so that it may bear more fruit. 3 You are already clean (pruned) because of the word which I have spoken to you. 4 **Abide in** Me, and I in you. As the branch cannot bear fruit of itself unless it **abides in** the vine, so neither can you unless you **abide in** Me. 5 I am the vine, you are the branches; he who **abides in** Me and I in him, he bears much fruit, for apart from Me you can do nothing. 6 If anyone does not **abide in** Me, he is thrown away as a branch and dries up; and they gather them and cast them into the fire and they are burned. 7 If you **abide in** Me, and My words **abide in** you, ask whatever you wish, and it will be done for you. 8 My Father is glorified by this, that you bear much fruit, and so prove to be My disciples.

Many think, if I fail to abide, I will be cast out and be cast into hell, but if I do abide I will bear much fruit, so I'd better start bearing fruit.

I better start producing fruit. Read it like this and Jesus' words will become a law for you: produce or perish. Jesus told the disciples; you are in me (meaning our imperfections are hidden in His perfection) the key verse is John 15:3 and the key words [already clean- past tense]and I am in you (we carry His sinless DNA as our own because we have already been purged [clean]). <u>Jesus didn't sin and we are hidden in Him</u>. This is talking about our new spirit man not our conduct (behaviour). If you let Him live His life through you, then without any conscious effort on your part you're going to start talking and acting just like sinless Jesus. This is a glorious promise for all who believe:

Whoever has been born of God does not sin, for His seed remains in him; and he cannot sin, because he has been born of God. 1 John 3:9 (sin is a noun, meaning a place, person, or thing) referring to your new spirit man.

So, what does it mean to abide in the vine? Here's the answer we've all been waiting for...

Whoever confesses that Jesus is the Son of God, **God abides in him, and he in God.** 1 John 4:15

But what about-Remain in me, and I will remain in you. John 15:4 NIV

Again, that sounds like a condition. It sounds like Jesus is saying, if your abiding performance is up to scratch, then I will reward you by abiding as well. <u>But it is not a condition to make us sweat; it is a promise to make us simply rest</u>.

If you read the rest of John 15 you will see how Jesus goes to great lengths to counter the law-mentality (performance-self effort) of the disciples. He does this by hitting them with promise after promise:

As the Father loved Me, I also have loved you; <u>abide in My love</u>. John 15:9

The reality is, **you are abiding in the vine because you have confessed Him as Lord**. But you may not be experiencing that reality. You may feel like you're not free or you're not abiding. Although you are a son or daughter with a permanent place in the family, seated at the Kings table, you may still think and act like the slave that you used to be. There's only one solution: **renew your mind!**

<u>Stop living by feelings and start walking by faith. You are abiding in fact, so start abiding in practice!</u>

God has revealed Himself in Scripture. Part of knowing God is to believe what He has revealed. Look up Colossians 1:15 –19.

<u>What does God reveal about Himself? Write down several major characteristics?</u>

Col 1:15-19 He is the image of the invisible God, the firstborn of all creation. 16 For by Him all things were created, both in the heavens and on earth, visible and invisible, whether thrones or dominions or rulers or authorities—all things have been created through Him and for Him. 17 He is before all things, and in Him all things hold together.

18 He is also head of the body, the church; and He is the beginning, the firstborn from the dead, so that He Himself will come to have first place in everything. 19 For it was the Father's good pleasure for all the fullness to dwell in Him,

-He (Jesus) is creator, the first.

-He (Jesus) holds all things together, Head of the body the Church, the being, the first born, will come to have first place in everything.

<u>What are some simple things that we can do to develop that relationship?</u>

One can commune with Him when ever, read the Word, listen to faith building grace-based sermons and teaching, worship etc

<u>What's the difference between knowing someone and only knowing about someone? And how does that apply to knowing God and not only knowing about God?</u>

An example would be for instance Prince William. We all have heard the name and seen pictures, but we have not met him, or have spent time with him as to have a relationship. The need to spend time and communicate (talk and listen).

"Let us occupy ourselves entirely in knowing God. The more we know Him, the more we will desire to know Him. As love increases with knowledge, the more we know God, the more we will truly love Him. We will learn to love Him equally in times of distress or in times of great joy." — Brother Lawrence, The Practice of the Presence of God

NOTES

WEEK THREE
The Goal

If God's free gift to all of humanity is eternal life (to know Him), then our ultimate goal should be to embrace that gift and bear fruit. In some ways, this section is an extension of last week's lesson. Now that we understand the essence of eternal life, we can accurately see the goal of the Christian life. It is important to remember its bearing fruit not producing fruit to recap part of last week's lesson.

<u>What is the goal of the Christian life?</u>

THE ULTIMATE GOAL IS TO KNOW GOD.

We embrace the gift of eternal life by getting to know God. It brings us back to our purpose in creation. We were created for relationship with God. To be sons and daughters. That takes us to our second goal. <u>How do you really get to know someone?</u>

What surpasses everything you'll ever do in the Christian life is the ability to be with Him - the ability to be one with Him is our present tense reality, we have our face unveiled as to know Him and to be known by Him. This truly is the greatest blessing of our lives. It isn't to serve the Lord although it is important that we do, but it's to know the Lord and our effortless response is simply doing what He does.

To know Him is eternal life. And it starts the very moment you're saved or born again because before that you were dead. You were created in the image of Adam. So, life begins through Christ the source of LIFE. Eternal life that produces everlasting life doesn't start when some trumpet blows, and Jesus comes or when you get to heaven one day.

It starts the very moment you get born again. And this eternal life is knowing Him which means; that you being born again is your introduction to relationship with God.

We're not applying principles to get results. It's not about following steps or formulas.

It is knowing that you're valuable to the heart of God, that you're loved by Him. Not because you've lovely, read your Bible or prayer for an hour, help some old person cross the road but because you know it because you've spent time with Him, expressing to Him (believing) and letting grace touch faith and mould you into that truth. That no matter the circumstances that come you know that you know you have favour with God. You know you're a child of God. A Son and a Daughter!

THE DAILY GOAL IS TO SPEND TIME WITH GOD.

As we saw last week, the only way we get to know someone is by spending time with that person. You can learn about a person through a book, but you can only get to know that person by spending time together. Let's expand on this thought out just a little more.

Think for a moment about dating. The primary purpose of dating is to get to know someone to see if you're compatible. While dating, you go where they go; you do what they do; you try to understand their heart, their character, their dreams, and plans. By spending time together, you discover their personality, mannerisms, etc. Over time, you get to know the person.

<u>Take that same approach to knowing God. How can you spend time with God?</u>

By communing, spending time in His presence, listening to faith building grace-based sermons etc

<u>Some common ways are?</u>

• Reading the Word (Bible) is a way to spend time with God and get to know Him is the primary was He also speaks to us. The Bible is God's revelation of Himself. In the Bible, God reveals His character, His heart, His desires, and His plans. The more you study the Bible, the better you know and understand God. In the next lesson we will deal with how to read the Word.

• Talking with God in prayer (communing) is a way to spend time with God and get to know Him. Prayer is not just telling God everything you need; prayer is also listening as God speaks to you. It takes time to discern God's voice in prayer. However, the more you're with Him, the more you will recognize His voice. Prayer is simply a conversation with our Heavenly Papa!

• Worshipping God is a way to spend time with God and get to know Him. Worship is not just singing. We worship God with our lives, our decisions, our actions, our pursuits and even in our giving. Worship can be as simple as focused reflection on God, offering thanks for what He's done, obeying His promptings and being just in AWE of who HE is!

• Listening to biblically Grace based new Covenant preaching and teaching is a way to spend time with God and get to know Him. Second Timothy 2:15 says, "Study to show ourselves approved to God." Christianity requires collaboration with other believers for relationships have always been His idea. As you listen to biblically based preaching and teaching, it points to Christ, to what He has already done this elevates Christ, encourages faith in Christ which in gives us confidence to share the truth of the Gospel to those around us.

• Time in nature can be a way to spend time with God and get to know Him. Romans 1 tells us that God's invisible attributes, nature, and character are clearly seen by what has been made. The Psalmist declares that the heavens are filled with the glory of God. While God's specific revelation of Himself is found in the Bible, God's general revelation can be seen in creation.

The goal is not just to know about God. The goal is not to become a biblical scholar. The goal is to know Him. You see, it is possible for a person to spend his or her entire life learning about God, doing spiritual things, but never really get to know Him.

The daily goal is to spend time with Him and not to feel condemned or guilty either when we don't. He is always with us He just want us to spend time with Him, HE wants to be involved in our daily living. Even in the small things and issues. We need to find ways to be with God and get to know Him.

<u>Based on the ways to spend time with God (found in this lesson), list several things you can start doing today.</u>

Purposely and not being religious about it but setting time aside to be alone with the Lord, reading the Word, praise and worshiping, listening to faith building grace-based teaching and sermon. Get a book or two a disc or two from the resource table etc

<u>If the goal is to know the God of the Bible, who can help you achieve that goal?</u>

The Pastor. A biblical mentor. Fellow believer. Sermons and Teaching that are faith building and grace-based etc

Sadly, many believers think that until you clean up your act perfectly and have just the right actions, God cannot have any relationship with you. That is anti-Gospel, and so contrary to the message Jesus brought. Romans 5:8 says" God commended His love toward you, and while you were yet a sinner, Christ died for you" so, the New Testament teaches that God extended His love to you while you were living in sin, not after you have cleaned up your act. One of the great truths of the Gospel that will change your life is to understand that God loves you just like you are.

He loves you so much that if you receive His love, you won't want to stay as you are. You will change, but you'll change as a by-product of God's love not in order to get His love.

Jesus has settled the sin issue on the Cross once and for all time and made you fully acceptable before the Father.

Write down these scriptures?

Romans 4:25 He was handed over to die because of our sins, and he was raised to life to make us right with God.

1 Peter 3:18 For Christ also died for sins once for all, the just for the unjust, so that He might bring us to God, having been put to death in the flesh, but made alive in the [a]spirit.

2 Cor 5:19-21 namely, that God was in Christ reconciling the world to Himself, not counting their trespasses against them, and He has committed to us the word of reconciliation. 20 Therefore, we are ambassadors for Christ, as though God were making an appeal through us; we beg you on behalf of Christ, be reconciled to God. 21 He made Him who knew no sin to be sin on our behalf, so that we might become the righteousness of God in Him.

Hebrews 9:25-28 And he did not enter heaven to offer himself again and again, like the high priest here on earth who enters the Most Holy Place year after year with the blood of an animal. 26 If that had been necessary, Christ would have had to die again and again, ever since the world began.

But now, once for all time, he has appeared at the end of the age to remove sin by his own death as a sacrifice.27 And just as each person is destined to die once and after that comes judgment, 28 so also Christ was offered once for all time as a sacrifice to take away the sins of many people. He will come again, not to deal with our sins, but to bring salvation to all who are eagerly waiting for him.

1 John 1:9 But if we confess our sins to him, he is faithful and just to forgive us our sins and to cleanse us from all unrighteousness (wickedness).

1 John 1:9 seems to contradict the other scripture above. <u>Should we be confessing's our sins</u>? Sin is stupid and has natural consequences, Rob a bank, go to jail. Sin is a substitute to that which is found authentic in the Father love. But A better question is whether Jesus will cleanse us from all sin or only some sin (specifically the sin we confess). <u>Does Jesus cleanse us from all unrighteousness or only some unrighteousness?</u> Here John the Apostle is unequivocal and clarifies it in the same letter. Jesus cleanses us from "**all unrighteousness**" (v.9). The blood of Jesus that was shed on the cross "**purifies us from all sin**" (v.7). And then, just in case we missed it, John says it a third time:

I write to you, dear children, <u>because your sins have been (past tense) forgiven on account of his name</u>. (1 John 2:12) Jesus doesn't just deal with the sin of your past, but the sin of your present and future as well. This is such great grace!

This is the revelation that will empower you to go and sin no more!

My little children, I am writing these things to you so that you may not sin. (1 John 2:1a) Confessing sins will not help you overcome sin, but grace will!

We don't confess to expunge (remove) sin, we confess to receive grace.

Big difference.

It is only the blood of Jesus that has remove sin, not our confessions.

If anyone sins, we have an Advocate with the Father, Jesus Christ the Righteous One. (1 John 2:1b)

NOTES

WEEK FOUR
How to Read your Bible

THE BIBLE IS GOD'S revelation of Himself, His LOVE letter and plan for redemption for all of humanity. Religions consists of man's thoughts about God, but the Bible isn't a compilation of men's thoughts—it contains God's thoughts.

We have developed a way of thinking based on our upbringing, experiences, circumstances, and the ungodly influences of this world rather than on the Word of God. Satan comes to steal and to deprive us of what God has given by challenging the way we think. This is evident even from his first dealings with mankind. Concerning the dangers of wrong thinking, the apostle Paul said,

But I fear, lest by any means, as the serpent beguiled Eve through his subtlety, so your minds should be corrupted from the simplicity that is in Christ. 2 Corinthians 11:3

When one does a study regarding that first encounter one sees the offering on enlightenment, ethical and moral living; religion. A form of Godliness. "God knows that your eyes will be opened (enlightenment) as soon as you eat it, and you will be like God, knowing both good and evil (ethical and Moral living)."

Genesis 3:5. Adam and Eve created in God image (likeness) were as godlike as they could have been, living from relationship alone and not from knowing what was good and what was not. But purely what was life (good) unconsciously because of intimacy through the source of life itself. The lie was sold that there was more, and the Father was withholding from them. And since then, man has been created in Adams image. Hence the need to be born again.

We hear people talk about "spiritual warfare" in the sense of going out and doing battle in the heavens. Praying for open heavens. This is based in a misunderstanding of a verse that says we are battling evil powers in heavenly, or high, places (Ephesians 6:11-12). Some people have actually chartered planes so they could "take their prayers to the sky," or they have gone to the top of skyscrapers to do battle "in heaven." This form of extreme intercession is not mentioned once in the New Testament. That isn't what this scripture is talking about. The battle against the enemy isn't somewhere out in the atmosphere; the battle is right between your ears.

Satan comes at you through thoughts with lies, deception, and distraction. Religion loves adding and subtracting from Gods Word just as with Adam and Eve. Here is an example.

We may eat of the fruit of the trees of the garden: But of the fruit of the tree, which is in the midst of the garden, God hath said, Ye shall not eat of it, neither shall ye touch it, lest ye die. Genesis 3:2-3. "but you must not eat from the tree of the knowledge of good and evil, for when you eat from it you will certainly die." Genesis 2:17.

The problem with what Eve said is that God never said they couldn't touch the fruit; He said don't eat it. This same thing is happening today. Religion has added to the Word of God and nullified it in order to hand down traditions. It's exactly what Jesus accused the scribes and the Pharisees of doing (Mark 7:13 thus invalidating (cancelling) the word of God by your tradition which you have handed down; and you do many things such as that"). Religion is always adding rules and regulations to the Word of God. It is saying, "Don't even touch it or you'll die!" Religion creates manmade traditions, and when people break the manmade traditions and don't die, they go ahead and break God's Word also, thinking that everything was just a big fat lie.

For example, some religious systems today are saying women shouldn't wear makeup or jewellery—which is a misunderstanding of the scripture that says women shouldn't be concerned with outward adorning, but rather be concerned with the beauty of their hearts. The scripture says don't be concerned with the "outward adorning of plaiting the hair, and of wearing of gold, or of putting on of apparel; But let it be the hidden man of the heart..." (1 Peter 3:3-4). If you interpret this to mean that there should be no plaiting of the hair or wearing of gold, then you have to say there shouldn't be any wearing of clothing either.

<u>Before we look at how to read the bible its vital that we also look at two other aspects. Is the bible trustworthy and how to rightly divide the Word of Truth?</u> Can we have confidence in the scriptures we have today as accurate?

It the Bible true?

All scripture is given by inspiration of God, and is profitable for doctrine, for reproof, for correction, for instruction in righteousness: That the man of God may be perfect, thoroughly furnished unto all good works. 2 Timothy 3:16-17

When the apostle Peter was getting toward the end of his life, he wrote a letter to believers in which he stressed the inspiration of Scripture and the confidence we can have that God is speaking to us through it. Peter knew that he was going to die shortly, and he was giving final encouragement to the believers. He said,

For we have not followed cunningly devised fables, when we made known unto you the power and coming of our Lord Jesus Christ, but were eyewitnesses of his majesty. For he received from God the Father honour and glory, when there came such a voice to him from the excellent glory, This is my beloved Son, in whom I am well pleased. And this voice which came from heaven we heard when we were with him in the holy mount. 2 Peter 1:16-18

Peter was saying, "My time here it at an end, but I'm going to write these things down so you can always have this to remember." He was making known that the account he gave of Jesus wasn't something he devised on his own. He wasn't just telling fables. The words he had written down were inspired by God, and they told of Peter's experiences.

Peter writes,

We have also a surer word of prophecy; whereunto ye do well that ye take heed, as unto a light that shineth in a dark place, until the day dawn, and the day star arise in your hearts: Knowing this first, that no prophecy of the scripture is of any private interpretation. For the prophecy came not in old time by the will of man: but holy men of God spake as they were moved by the Holy Spirit. 2 Peter 1:19-21

Peter saw Moses and Elijah talk with Jesus on the Mount of Transfiguration. He saw Jesus radiate light, and he heard God speak with an audible voice from heaven and confirm that Jesus was His Son, but he says we have something even better than that—better than seeing with our eyes or hearing with our ears—we have the written Word of God!

Peter clearly states that the Word of God was not written by men—it was not of "any private interpretation." The Holy Spirit inspired men to write the scriptures. The apostle Paul made the same point in his letter to Timothy when he said,

All scripture is given by inspiration of God, and is profitable for doctrine, for reproof, for correction, for instruction in righteousness: That the man of God may be perfect, thoroughly furnished unto all good works. 2 Timothy 3:16-17

The Greek word for "given by inspiration of God" is literally translated "divinely breathed." This clearly states that the Word of God didn't come from the thoughts of men.

God breathed His thoughts into men, who then put them in writing. The Bible is not a human book; it's God's book written for men (mankind).

To begin with, the manuscript evidence supporting the New Testament far outstrips any evidence for secular writings of ancient times.

<u>The New Testament documents have more manuscripts, earlier manuscripts, and more abundantly supported manuscripts than the best ten pieces of classical literature combined.</u>

In contrast to the copies of secular histories given, more than 5,600 Greek manuscripts of the New Testament have survived in whole or in part. Those manuscripts vary in age, the more complete having been written within 150 years of the original, with the earliest manuscript portion written within 30 years of the original. (Keep in mind that the New Testament wasn't written as a single book but is composed of many letters written by multiple authors at different times.)

From a purely human perspective, the chance for error is increased when a document is copied over-and-over again thousands of times. The more times something is copied, the more errors you should see. This is true in the case of secular works, but not with the Bible. The abundance of ancient New Testament manuscripts has been compared and there are very few differences—and they contain no differences whatsoever that contradict the Gospel message of Jesus or the historical facts of Christian faith. Scholars have placed the comparative accuracy between the more than 5,600 manuscripts at 99.5%!

In addition to the Greek copies of the New Testament, there are thousands more copies of New Testament books produced in other languages during the same time frame. In fact, researchers have discovered more than 9,000 copies of New Testament manuscripts in other languages—bringing the total number of manuscripts to well over 14,000. The abundance of ancient manuscripts and the nearness of their composition to the actual events, makes the New Testament the most verifiable document of antiquity.

Not only do we have copies of the scriptures themselves, but leaders in the early Christian church (often called the Church Fathers) wrote prolifically between 90 and 160 A.D. Their familiarity with the New Testament scriptures we still read today is proven by the fact that all but 11 verses from the New Testament are quoted in their writings!

Non-Christians have also given evidence of Jesus as a historical figure in their writings. In 93 A.D., the Jewish historian Flavius Josephus wrote about the persecution and death of James. He said that the Sanhedrin "...brought before them the brother of Jesus, who was called Christ, whose name was James, and some others, [or, some of his companions]; and when he had formed an accusation against them as breakers of the law, he delivered them to be stoned."

The discovery of the Dead Sea Scrolls between 1946 and 1957 in several caves on the shores of the Dead Sea has given us further evidence of the accuracy of the Scriptures that have been handed down to us.

Among the Dead Sea Scrolls was an intact copy of the entire book of Isaiah (known as the Great Isaiah Scroll).

It is dated at 100 B.C. and is 1000 years older than the copies that were used to compose the book of Isaiah we read in our Bibles today. Miniscule, with the variations consisting mostly of spelling mistakes and simple copying errors. The discovery of the Dead Sea Scrolls also proves that the Messianic prophecies we read in Isaiah were definitely written prior to the birth of Jesus, which reinforces the case that Scripture makes for Jesus as the Messiah.

The bottom line is that the Bible has been handed down through the ages with such accuracy that it can't be just a mere book. The different copies we have of ancient secular writings have significant differences in them because men simply copied them—they weren't inspired and preserved by God. The Bible, on the other hand, has been supernaturally preserved by God and all of the evidence we have supports that it was written by the inspiration of God. The last words of David, king of Israel and author of the Messianic prophecies in Psalm 22, reveal how the Holy Spirit inspired the men who wrote Scripture. The Word is reliable!

Jesus quoted from the Septuagint, which was a Greek translation of the Hebrew Old Testament, and He equated Scripture with words proceeding from the mouth of God (see ref. Matthew 4:4). Jesus' use of Scripture throughout the Gospels also shows that He believed it was the final authority.

Additionally, Paul the Apostle hinged his letter to the Galatians on the fact that God made His promise to the seed (singular) of Abraham, instead of to his seeds (plural) (see ref. Galatians 3:16).

Paul made an argument for Jesus as the promised seed of Abraham based on the singular form of one word from a translation of the original Old Testament scripture—which shows that God is well able to preserve the truth in His Word for us, even though translations!

How do I study the Bible?

One way we should not read the Word is by simply using our finger and wherever it land take that scripture as if it is speaking directly to us.

There are several keys to keep in mind while studying the Bible.

1. The Holy Spirit Enables Our Understanding

"But when He, the Spirit of truth, comes, He will guide you into all the truth; for He will not speak on His own initiative, but whatever He hears, He will speak; and He will disclose to you what is to come" (John 16:13).

If you don't understand ask the Helper (Holy Spirit) to bring you understanding and revelation. The Word confirms the Spirit, and the Spirit the Word. They will never contradict themselves.

2. Let Scripture Interprets Scripture

"But know this first of all, that no prophecy of Scripture is a matter of one's own interpretation, for no prophecy was ever made by an act of human will, but men moved by the Holy Spirit spoke from God" (2 Peter 1:20–21).

Here is an example Mat 5:18. "For verily I say unto you, till heaven and earth pass, one jot or one tittle shall in no wise pass from the law." Many would see this as proof that enforces the Old Covenant Law (including the 10 Commandments) but what they fail to realize is that the verse quoted is not complete. The actual verse reads - "For verily I say unto you, Till heaven and earth pass, one jot or one tittle shall in no wise pass from the law, till all be fulfilled." Mat 5:18. To rightly divide the Word of Truth we need to submit a verse to the rest of Scripture. But what does the rest of scripture say when we don't allow scripture to interpret scripture. In the book of the Acts, we find a commentary on the word "**fulfil**" as used in Matt. 5:17.

Acts 13:15 "The law and the prophets.", vs 20 "Until Samuel the prophet, vs 25 "John **fulfilled** his course.", vs 33 The promise had been "**fulfilled.**", vs 39 "The law of Moses.". To "fulfil" means to reach the end of the prediction. It has been completed – not to repeated. The following passages show clearly how the word is used in the Scriptures "Until the times of the Gentiles be **fulfilled**." (Luke 21:24), "And as John **fulfilled** his course."(Acts 13:25), "What shall be the sigh when all these things shall be fulfilled?" (Mark 13:4.),"The voices of the prophets, they have **fulfilled**." (Acts 13:27.), "And when they had **fulfilled** all that was written of him." (Acts 13: 29.), "The promise, which was made unto the fathers, God hath **fulfilled**." (Acts 13: 32, 33.). After this manner, then, Jesus came to **"fulfil"** all that had been written concerning himself -"**All things must be fulfilled**, which were written in the law of Moses, and in the prophets, and in the psalms, concerning me." (Luke 24:44.) Another great point is that the term heaven and earth was in reference to the Jewish temple as it was known!

3. Context Unlocks Meaning (Context - Text = Con after all)

Example. "There is NO God." Psalms 14:1 says, "There is no God." BUT is that what the context implies? No, the context of this verse reads "Fools say in their hearts, 'There is no God.' They are corrupt, they do abominable deeds; there is no one who does good." (Psalm 14:1). Can you see the danger of just pulling a verse out of its context? It can result in saying the exact opposite of what the Scripture says. Taken out of context, this quote says there is no God. But the context around this verse is not saying this at all.

4. The Original scriptures were never had chapters and verses

The placement of Chapters came about when Stephen Langton, Archbishop of Canterbury in the early 13th century and professor at the University of Paris, added chapter numbers to all of the books in 1227AD. They've stuck ever since.

In 1551AD, a printer by the name of Robert Stephanus, added verses to the text of the New Testament within the chapter divisions as he was riding on horseback from Paris to Lyons.

5. Audience

For instance, is this passage written to the Jew, the Gentile, the Church, the believer, the unbeliever, is it in the past tense, present tense, or future tense.

For example, it is important to note for instance that the book of Romans presents an essential theme of justification by faith alone and not by works. The book of Hebrews was written primarily for the Jewish law keepers and emphasis was on contrast of the old into the far better new covenants.

In the Book of Galatians was written primarily for legalists (Judaizers) in the church, that were teaching that Old Testament laws were still binding upon Christians, and that God's promises extended only to Jews, and that Gentiles must be circumcised before they could fully experience salvation. This was in direct contradiction to Paul's the Apostles insistence that salvation was by grace through faith alone.

The emphasis was that righteousness is not of works or the law. Christ fulfilled the law for us, as we could not do it. That Christ is the source of grace, truth, and righteousness, and all of this is available to us through faith in Christ alone and not any other means.

6. Through the lens of the NEW COVENANT

We should be careful not to mix the Old Covenant with the New Covenant.

The New Covenant does not start – where it says: "New Testament" in your bible. The blank paper is not the separating factor. It starts after Christs miraculous and powerful resurrection after His death on the Cross.

This is the dividing moment in History that the enemy was defeated, and everything change. So, this lens considers what is before and what is after this victory.

Not everything written in the old testament is old covenant just as not everything written in the new is new covenant. If not, you will not have a clear picture of all that Christ has accomplish on the Cross.

After all, the DEATH and RESURRECTION changed everything.......and just as Christ said that Moses and the Prophets spoke of Him, we are to search the Old looking for our saviour. No longer looking for the shadows but the substance. Which is our reality. And view all the old through the lens of Christ and His finished works.

Example, what is commonly known as the Lord's Prayer we read in Matthew 6:13 And lead us not into temptation but deliver us from the evil one.' 14 For if you forgive men their trespasses, your Heavenly Father will also forgive you. 15 But if you do not forgive men their trespasses, neither will your Father forgive yours....This is an incredible thing so many overlook. In essence this is saying that God will only forgive you in proportion to how you have forgiven. Praise God for the new and far better covenant we have. We know this is prior (pre-cross) to the new covenant because the Cross and resurrection had not taken place. Now after the Cross Paul the Apostle reminds us in Ephesians 4:3 Instead, be kind to each other, tender-hearted, <u>forgiving one another, just as God through Christ has forgiven you.</u>

No longer is God forgiving us based on how we forgave but we forgive because we are the forgiven.

7. The Ultimate Goal Is to Know Him

The ultimate goal for studying the Bible is not knowledge, or memorising scripture. The goal for studying the Bible is to know God. To see Jesus in every scripture. Both in the new and the old because all scripture speaks of Him.

You examine the Scriptures carefully because you suppose that in them you have eternal life. Yet they testify about me. John 5:39

And having begun from Moses and from all the Prophets, He (Jesus) interpreted to them the things concerning Himself in all the Scriptures. Luke 24:27

NOTES

WEEK FIVE
Baptisms

WATER BAPTISM

Do I need to be baptized to go to Heaven? NO

Do I need to be baptized to be a member of this Church? NO

Do I need to be baptized if I was baptized as a baby? Yes and NO. To be baptized means to be fully submerged and there are some requirements. No, you don't have to you get too.

Baptism requirements. One requirement is **repentance**. Repentance does not mean turning from sin but changing your mind- turning away from sin may be immediate or it may be a process, but it is not a requirement for repentance. Otherwise coming to Christ is based on your efforts (works-based) and not by faith. Did you have a change of heart and a change of mind that resulted in turning from sin to Jesus and His forgiveness (Acts 2:38 Peter said to them, "Repent, and each of you be baptized in the name of Jesus Christ for the forgiveness of your sins; and you will receive the gift of the Holy Spirit, Acts 20:21 solemnly testifying to both Jews and Greeks of repentance toward God and faith in our Lord Jesus Christ , and Acts 17:30 Therefore having overlooked the times of ignorance, God is now declaring to men that all people everywhere should repent) <u>Did you exercise faith in Jesus as your Lord and Savior?</u>

(Mark 16:16 He who has believed and has been baptized shall be saved; but he who has disbelieved shall be condemned, John 3:16 For God so loved the world, that He gave His only begotten Son, that whoever believes in Him shall not perish, but have eternal life. 17 For God did not send the Son into the world to judge the world, but that the world might be saved through Him. 18 He who believes in Him is not judged; he who does not believe has been judged already, because he has not believed in the name of the only begotten Son of God, [always good to read to verse 18] and Rom. 10:9-10 that if you confess with your mouth Jesus as Lord, and believe in your heart that God raised Him from the dead, you will be saved; 10 for with the heart a person believes, resulting in righteousness, and with the mouth he confesses, resulting in salvation.) If not, then turn to Jesus now, repent, turn to His grace to forgive you, and seal that decision to follow Him through water baptism.

You see, Water Baptism is an act that expresses one's faith in Jesus. Without that faith, the act means nothing. People who turned to Jesus as Lord and Savior were willing to express that faith and openly confess Jesus in this public way. People who say "no" to Jesus' command are showing, to some extent, a dead faith. Faith is dead when people are unwilling to express it (James 2:18 But someone may well say, "You have faith and I have works; show me your faith without the works, and I will show you my faith by my works." Faith alone saves by grace, but saving faith is never alone. It is always willing to express itself. Baptism is a way of expressing that faith. Baptism is not what saves; it is Jesus. Just as it is not a prayer that saves but Jesus.

Water baptism doesn't wash away sins; it is only the blood of Jesus that has. But faith applies His blood to you, and sometimes that faith was expressed at the time a person was baptized (Acts 22:16 Now why do you delay? Get up and be baptized, and wash away your sins, calling on His name). Baptism is knowing that you have died in Christ but that you have also been risen in Christ. That the old You died on the Cross in Christ and the new You (spirit man) where raise in Christ at the resurrection as we learnt in lesson 1. This change that took place when you were born again was in your spirit man, not your soul or body.

<u>The question is, have you repented? Do you believe in Him (Jesus)?</u> Do you understand what Jesus accomplished on the Cross and you are in Him and He in You. If so, why delay—arise and be baptized!

Also, baptism is a sign of the new covenant just as communion is. Although communion can be done as often as one likes, true water baptism is a one-time event.

You don't need to do a special training course to be baptized. You do not need to make yourself ready over many weeks, month or years to be baptized. "Repent, and be baptized..." (see Acts 2:38) can and should be a secondary event immediately following the primary event – that of repentance.

The decision to be baptized most often is spontaneous. The eunuch said to Philip: "Look, here is water. What can stand in the way of my being baptized?" (see Acts 8:36)

Baptism in water does not have to be carried out by a Pastor or even by a church leader, just as the laying on of hands for a person to receive Christ or to receive the Baptism of the Holy Spirit does not have to be carried out by a Pastor or leader of a church. "Those that accepted his message were baptized, and about three thousand were added to their numbers that day." (See Acts 2:41). So many were baptized in one day that it is clear that they were not baptized exclusively by Peter and the apostles.

Baptism is full immersion in water. It is not a sprinkle of water on your forehead and not to be confused with baby dedication. The same word used for baptism is the same word used for pickling pickles, and the same word for dying clothes.

Baptism is the physical manifestation of the spiritual truth that at the time of us being born again, we were buried (note the past tense) with Christ into death, to be raised up into His (victorious and abundant) life. "We were therefore buried with Him through baptism into death, in order that, just as Christ was raised from the dead through the Glory of the father, we too may walk in newness of life." (See Romans 6:4)

For those interest in being water baptized please get in contact with your local church if required.

The Baptism of the Holy Spirit

What is the difference between being born again and the baptism of the Holy Spirit?

We see in the book of Acts separate experiences from that of being born again. In one instance, Philip was preaching in the city of Samaria, and the entire city believed. (see Acts 8:4-8) During that time Philip performed many miracles, but then we read the following in Acts 8:14-17 "Now when the apostles in Jerusalem heard that Samaria had received the word of God, they sent them Peter and John, who came down and prayed for them that they might receive the Holy Spirit. For He had not yet fallen upon any of them; they had simply been baptized in the name of the Lord Jesus. Then they began laying their hands on them, and they were receiving the Holy Spirit.

Again, we see another example of a second born again experience this time with Paul the Apostle in Acts 19:1-7 it happened that while Apollos was at Corinth, Paul passed through the upper country and came to Ephesus, and found some disciples. He said to them, "Did you receive the Holy Spirit when you believed?" And they said to him, "No, we have not even heard whether there is a Holy Spirit." And he said, "Into what then were you baptized?" And they said, "into John's baptism." Paul said, "John baptized with the baptism of repentance, telling the people to believe in Him who was coming after him, that is, in Jesus." When they heard this, they were baptized in the name of the Lord Jesus. And when Paul had laid his hands upon them, the Holy Spirit came on them, and they began speaking with tongues and prophesying. There were in all about twelve men.

It's pretty clear that there are two different events in scripture after the day of Pentecost. One of being born again and the other the baptism of the Holy Spirit. In essence it's the Holy Spirit that baptizes us into the Body of Christ and at baptism its Christ who baptizes us into the Holy Spirit.

If I speak in the tongues of men and of angels, but have not love, I am a noisy gong or a clanging cymbal. 1 Cor 13:1

<u>You might be thinking but wait didn't I get all of the Holy Spirits ability when I received Jesus being born again</u>? You receive the Holy Spirit when you are born again, because you can't have the Spirit of God in you in order to be born again (1 Cor. 12:13 For by one Spirit we were all baptized into one body, whether Jews or Greeks, whether slaves or free, and we were all made to drink of one Spirit). You are sealed by the Holy Spirit, approved, and enclosed becoming the temple of the Holy Spirit. (1 Cor 6:19) So, if you don't speak in tongues or prophesy you are not any less saved, than those that do. We have to cooperate with the Holy Spirit for He will never force Himself on anyone. He is the perfect gentleman!

At the new birth our nature changes. At the baptism in the Holy Spirit our ability changes!

<u>Tongues.</u> Speaking in tongues is still valid and I would go as far as saying it is a necessity in a Christian wanting to live the victorious life. Speaking in tongues is a grace gift, a manifestation of the Holy Spirits power in us after we have received the baptism of the Holy Spirit. It is when the

Holy Spirit inspires our spirit to pray to God, using the same vocal cords we use to speak. Making sounds our natural minds can't comprehend. (1 Cor. 14:2 For one who speaks in a tongue does not speak to men but to God; for no one understands, but in his spirit he speaks mysteries.). We see in every instance that when the Baptism of the Holy spirit was received there was evidence of speaking in tongues. Every time.

Tongues can be the supernatural speaking of a heavenly language (see 1 Cor. 13:1), or the supernatural speaking of a human language that is unknown to the speaker. (see Acts 2:1-13)

<u>But why should I speak in tongues</u>? Am I not going to be like a puppet and the Holy Spirit the puppet Master? Speaking in tongues build's your faith (see Jude 20). It also helps to draw out into your natural mind the wisdom that is in your Born-Again spirit man, which is just like Jesus. Your Spirit Man contains the mind of Christ (1 Cor 2:16 For who has known the mind of the Lord, that he will instruct Him? But we have the mind of Christ) and knows all things (1 John 2:20) and speaking in tongues draws it out. Speaking in tongues also brings a supernatural rest and refreshing. (see Is. 28:11-12) and will enable us to give thanks to God way above our natural limits our natural tongue. (1 Cor 14:15-17 What is the outcome then? I will pray with the spirit, and I will pray with the mind also; I will sing with the spirit, and I will sing with the mind also. 16 Otherwise if you bless [a]in the spirit only, how will the one who fills the place of the [b]ungifted say the "Amen" at your giving of thanks, since he does not know what you are saying? 17 For you are giving thanks well enough, but the other person is not edified).

<u>What are some Hindrances to speaking in tongues?</u> One hinderance is simply a lack of knowledge (revelation) and another is simply unbelief. If God who is good how would not any gift from Him not be good. Sadly, many have been taught wrongly regarding tongues and in that have replace a lie with truth. As stated earlier not speaking in tongues

does not mean you are not saved or that you will instantly speak in the tongue of angels when you received the baptism of the Holy Spirit. I myself received the baptism of the Holy Spirit but only spoke in tongues several months later due to a renewing of the mind and replacing the lie with truth.

<u>How long should I pray in the Spirit</u>? It's about knowing Him. Do you say to you loved one how much time do I need to spend with you? An hour, two maybe. No, we are always in the Spirit even when we don't speak in tongues. Yes, it's important to spend time, as Paul the Apostle stated in 1 Cor 14:18, "I thank God that I speak in tongues more than all of you." And we know from the context of Chapter 14 that he was referring to speaking in the tongues of angels. (1 Cor 14:2 For one who speaks in a tongue does not speak to men but to God; for no one understands, but in his spirit he speaks mysteries).

<u>How does speaking in tongues work?</u> Just as with salvation God does not make you receive. He isn't going to make you speak in tongues.

God does not take over peoples' bodies. It's not a shot-gun wedding. You can't just open your mouth and wait for a sound to come out. As you begin to utter words the Holy Spirit is inspiring you to speak, the words will come out more and more easily. You won't understand and it will sound like nonsense but keep at it. The natural mind can't understand what is spiritual (1 Cor 2:14 But a natural man does not accept the things of the Spirit of God, for they are foolishness to him; and he cannot understand them, because they are spiritually appraised.) but one can ask for an interpretation (1 Cor 14:13 Therefore let one who speaks in a tongue pray that he may interpret.). Getting an interpretation does not mean a word for word translation, it could be that in the future God will give you a word of knowledge or wisdom. The only time an interpretation is required immediately is during a church service. It is not necessary when praying privately.

How do we receive the Baptism of the Holy Spirit?

There is only one requirement to receiving the baptism of the Holy Spirit.

You need to be born again. Jesus does all the work. In the same way you believed when Jesus came to live in you. You simply believed the Good News and gave voice to your declaration of belief.

He is the one that baptizes you into the Holy Spirit (see ref. Matt 3:11), so if you have not it would be our great pleasure to do so.

Let us all pray this together believing in our hearts for this incredible grace gift that will empower us to life the victorious Christian life.

"Father, I thank you that I am the Temple of the Holy Spirit, I welcome You to fill me right now. Thank You for filling me with your presence.

Amen!"

NOTES

WEEK SIX
The New Covenant

———

However miraculous the birth of Jesus is and the many prophecies regarding His birth, it is in fact <u>His death that is the single most Significant event for all Christianity</u>, God Himself looks at the cross as the dividing line of redemptions plan and the new way He has choose to deal with all mankind.

You see how He dealt with mankind before the cross is very different from how He deals with you and me today. Before the cross, God dealt with man based on full compliance of obedience to the law. To the Jew they had the written Law of Moses. To the Gentile they had the Law written on their conscience/mind through the knowledge of good and evil. But today beloved, God deals with mankind based on His love and grace.

The reason for the change is that **Christ's death ushered in a brand-new covenant**. This new covenant that has been prophesied throughout the Old Testament, and the day Christ died, His blood was shed, and He arose it went into effect as the new way of How God would relate to us.

A covenant is the same word for a testament, agreement or will. For a will or covenant to go into effect, the one who made it must die.

Most of us understand this from our legal systems. If you have a will, it will not go into effect until you die.

This is what the Author of Hebrews brings to light in chapter 9:16-17 which says: In the case of a will, it is necessary to prove the death of the one who made it, because a will is in force only when somebody has died; it never takes effect while the one who made it is living. Therefore, <u>for the new covenant that God had promised to go into effect, Christ had to die.</u>

The Old Covenant of the Law

This new covenant is completely different from the covenant that God had established with Moses and the nation of Israel at Mt. Sinai. It is not a renewed agreement but a complete new one.

"For the law was given by Moses, but grace and truth came by Christ." (John 1;17)

After being in bondage and slavery for four hundred years, God led the Israelites out of Egypt and through the Red Sea remembering the agreement He had made with Abraham (Ex 2:24 God heard their groaning and He remembered His covenant with Abraham, with Isaac and with Jacob.). The Israelites camped at Mt. Sinai and their God gave them the Law. This covenant was a conditional agreement. If they would fully obey Him and keep all the laws He set before them (613 of them which includes the Ten Commandments), then they would be His treasured possession...and a holy nation (Exodus 19:5-6 Now if you obey me fully and keep my covenant, then out of all nations you will be my treasured possession. Although the whole earth is mine, 6 you[a] will be for me a kingdom of priests and a holy nation.' These are the words you are to speak to the Israelites.)

"Then all the people answered together and said, "All that the LORD has spoken we will do.""

So, Moses brought back the words of the people to the LORD as its mediator. And the LORD said to Moses, "Behold, I come to you in the thick cloud, that the people may hear when I speak with you, and believe you forever." So, Moses told the words of the people to the LORD. Then the LORD said to Moses, "Go to the people and consecrate them today and tomorrow, and let them wash their clothes. And let them be ready for the third day. For on the third day the LORD will come down upon Mount Sinai in the sight of all the people. You shall set bounds for the people all around, saying, 'Take heed to yourselves that you do not go up to the mountain or touch its base. Whoever touches the mountain shall surely be put to death. Not a hand shall touch him, but he shall surely be stoned or shot with an arrow; whether man or beast, he shall not live.' When the trumpet sounds long, they shall come near the mountain.'" (Exodus 19:8-13)

Their response reveals the heart of man's self-righteousness in his belief that he has the ability to produce righteousness by his own ability. And from that moment forth, God changed His tone, No longer would He be merciful to the murmuring and complaining. No more would He be gracious to speak to them face to face but now behind a veil and through a mediator. The children of Israel should never have changed the covenant that brought them out of Egypt, the Abrahamic agreement. For under the agreement of The Law, the Law condemns the best of us but is unable to help us. As we will see later on, this is the very purpose of the Law in our lives. It is a tutor or school master to lead us to the revelation that we need a savior.

To seal this covenant, Moses and the Israelites offered burnt offerings and sacrificed young bulls to the Lord:

When Moses had proclaimed every commandment of the law to all the people, he took the blood of calves, together with water, scarlet wool, and branches of hyssop, and sprinkled the scroll and all the people. He said, "This is the blood of the covenant, which God has commanded you to keep." Hebrews 9:19-20

The sign of this covenant agreement would be the keeping of the Sabbath day. (Ezek 20:12 Also I gave them my Sabbaths as a sign between us, so they would know that I the Lord made them holy.)

However, before Moses could get down to bring the commands, the Israelites had already built a golden calf, saying "These are your gods, O Israel, who brought you up out of Egypt" (Exodus 32:4).

They could not keep the first commandment. This very commandant they promise to surely do with ease for whatever was commanded they could do. You see the Israelites could not live up to the covenant. And for the breaking of the agreement the very first day the Law was given 3000 were killed (see Exodus 32:28 The Levites did as Moses commanded, and that day about three thousand of the people died.). In Duet 28 we see a list of both blessing and curses that was fully dependent on perfect obedience. Twice as many curses for being disobedient.

Moses being angry with the people, broke the two tablets of stone, and then had to return to the mountain to receive a replacement set of two tablets onto which the commandments were rewritten by God.

(Deuteronomy 10:1-2)

The 3,000 dying at Mount Sinai due to the (immediate) application of the Old Testament law - which was the "ministry of death", is contrasted with the 3,000 coming into eternal life and being filled with the Holy Spirit on the day of Pentecost (see Acts 2:41) though the powerful and superior "ministry of grace and truth".

The law demands perfection, it is unbending and immoveable but won't lift a hand to help. Because we are all born in sin, Adams sin- it is impossible for anyone to live up to the righteous requirements. But God's intent was not for us to try to live up to the law and its perfect standard.

His intent was to show us our sinfulness and our need for salvation. And this is all the Old Covenant can show us. It is like a mirror; it can show you the dirt on your face but is unable to clean it. There is nothing wrong with the law. Paul the Apostle wrote, the law is holy, and the commandment is holy, righteous, and good (Romans 7:10). The problem was not with the Law. The problem is with us. As Hebrews 8:7 says, "For if there had been nothing wrong with that first covenant, no place would have been sought for another. But God found fault with the people."

While teaching about God's holy nature, the law also revealed how unholy and unrighteous we are. Paul the Apostle explained his own experience while living under the Law:

Indeed, I would not have known what sin was except through the law. For I would not have known what coveting really was if the law had not said, "Do not covet". But sin, seizing the opportunity afforded by the commandment, produced in me every kind of covetous desire... Romans 7:7-8

Therefore, no one will be declared righteous in His sight by observing the law; rather, through the law, we become conscious of sin. Romans 3:20

The Law is Holy but when it flows through man's sinful flesh, it shows just how utterly sinful we truly are. The Law is holy, but it cannot make us holy. The Law reveals who we are, but it cannot remove our blemishes. We simply cannot live up to the stringent unbending requirements of the 613 demands.

Paul the Apostle discovered something else about the law; "the very commandment that was intended to bring life actually brought death" (Romans 7:12). Coupled with the commandments is punishment for a violation. Death. That right under the law, the punishment for sin is death: For the wages of sin is death (Romans 6:23). Because of this there is no hope under this old covenant. That is one thing that the Law does: It create in you, hopelessness, and the revelation that you need a savior.

"Therefore the law was our tutor to bring us to Christ, that we might be justified by faith. But after faith has come, we are no longer under a tutor."

Galatians 3:24-25

For it is impossible to keep, the more we try the more we fail. It condemned us. That's what the Old Covenant does. It revealed our sinful nature before we are born again and showed us how far we are from God's standard of holiness that we would need a savior.

This is why Paul the Apostle described the old covenant as the ministry of condemnation, and the ministry of death (2 Cor. 3:90. If the ministry that brought condemnation was glorious, how much more glorious is the ministry that brings righteousness! 2 Cor 3:7 Now if the ministry that brought death, which was engraved in letters on stone, came with glory, so that the Israelites could not look steadily at the face of Moses because of its glory, transitory though it was).

It was a covenant that required man to live up to its righteous standards perfectly, and to those who failed it said, the wages of sin is death. Because man could not live up to the requirements of the old covenant, he experienced fear, shame, condemnation and guilt, and the result was one could never draw near to God. One hid from Him!

That is where the Old Mosaic Covenant leaves us, but God had spoken of a new covenant coming. In Jeremiah 31 verse 31-32 "The day is coming," says the Lord, "when I will make a new covenant with the people of Israel and Judah.

This covenant will not be like the one I made with their ancestors when I took them by the hand and brought them out of the land of Egypt.

Something way better was coming. The writer of Hebrews puts it this way:

<u>The former regulation is set aside because it was weak and useless (for the law made nothing perfect), and a better hope is introduced, by which we draw near to God</u>. Hebrews 7:18,19

The Old agreement vs. The New Agreement

That 'better hope' is found in the New Covenant. In contrast to the Old Covenant, it is a covenant of grace (God unmerited and undeserving Favour), not of law. The following passage of scripture will help us to see the differences between the two.

<u>The law is only a shadow of the good things that are coming – not the realities themselves.</u>

For this reason, it can never, by the same sacrifices repeated endlessly year after year, make perfect those who draw near to worship. If it could, would they not have stopped being offered? For the worshipers would have been cleansed once for all, and would no longer have felt guilty for their sins. But those sacrifices are an annual reminder of sins, because it is impossible for the blood of bulls and goats to take away sins. Hebrews 10:1-4

The forgiveness of sins under the Old Covenant was a <u>good news/bad news situation</u>. Each year, on the Day of Atonement, the High Priest entered the Holy of Holies to sprinkle the blood of a bull on the mercy seat to cover the sins of the people committed during the previous year.

Then two goats were sacrificed. One was slain at the altar, the other served as the scapegoat. The sins of the people were transferred symbolically to the scapegoat. And then it was driven out of the city, out into the wilderness, symbolizing the removal of the people's sins. That was the good news.

The bad news was that the next day a person's sins began piling up again. And with that came their shame, guilt, and condemnation. That they could not draw near to the Father. Next year another sacrifice. Year after year, after year...and so the cycle went.

God graciously gave this system to Israel as a means for them to experience some relief from their shame, guilt, and condemnation. But these sacrifices only covered sins temporarily, but they could not take them away forever. Under the Old Covenant, man could enjoy the blessing of God's forgiveness, but that system provided no final solution to the sin issue.

That is why the law is only a shadow. It is a picture of Christ and His finished work on our behalf. It was not the reality. Once you have the real thing, there is no longer a need to focus on the shadow.

Under the New Covenant, Jesus died for sin once for all. He did not cover our sins like the sacrifices under the law did. He was the Lamb of God who took away our sins.

Therefore, when Christ came into the world, He said: "Sacrifice and offering you did not desire, but a body you prepared for Me; with burnt offerings and sin offerings you were not pleased. Then I said, 'Here I am' it is written about Me in the scroll I have come to do your will, O God." First he said, "Sacrifices and offerings, burnt offerings and sin offerings you did not desire, nor were you pleased with them" (although the law required them to be made). Then he said, "Here I am, I have come to do Your will." He sets aside the first to establish the second. Hebrews 10:5-

Although the law required sin offerings to be made, they could never pay the price for sin. All they could do was cover them for a year.

In order for sin to be fully paid for and taken away, there had to be a perfect payment, a perfect sacrifice from a perfect lamb. This is the primary reason Christ came into the world. He offered Himself as a spotless lamb that would take away the sins of the world. As a result, there is no longer any need to offer sacrifices.

He restored back that which was lost. We are now once again friends of God and sons and daughters of God. You see God has set aside the old covenant to establish a new and better covenant.

And by that will, we have been made holy through the sacrifice of the body of Jesus Christ once for all. Day after day every priest stands and performs his religious duties; again, and again he offers the same sacrifices, which can never take away sins. But when this priest had offered for all time one sacrifice for sins, he sat down at the right hand of God. Since that time, he waits for His enemies to be made his footstool, because by one sacrifice he has made perfect forever... Hebrews 10:10-14

The New Covenant sacrifice was perfect because Jesus was/is: The perfect sacrificial lamb of God; the eternal Priest called by God; and Jesus is eternally part of the God Head. So, God laid down His life (Jesus) for our benefit. We did not contribute to this powerful life-giving sacrifice, just as Abraham did not contribute to His amazing covenant with God.

He fell asleep and God (it should have been Abraham) walked between the bleeding pieces of split animals. (See Gen. 15:12 and Gen. 15:17)

"Called by God as High Priest, according to the order of Melchizedek" (Hebrews 5:10).

Being unworthy, we did not partake or have any part in the sacrifice. This means that our behavior, sins, or sacrifices, can have no effect on what has already occurred perfectly and independently from us.

However, when we are born again, by faith, we participate in being fully crucified with Christ unto death and raised up in newness of His life. (see Romans 6:4-5)

One thing you would never find in an Old Testament temple is a chair. The reason is that a priest's job was never ever finished. Since the sacrifices offered could never take away sin, they had to continually be offered to keep covering sins. But when Christ offered Himself once and for all, He said, "It is finished." He then sat down at the right hand of God. We have been made holy, righteous, sanctified, accepted, and perfect forever through His final sacrifice. There is nothing left to offer God as a payment for sin.

The Holy Spirit also testified to us about this. First, He says: "This is the covenant I will make with them after that time, says the Lord. I will put my laws (not talking about the Ten Commandments here) in their hearts, and I will write them on their minds." Then he adds: "Their sins and lawless acts I will remember no more." And where these have been forgiven, there is no longer any sacrifice for sin. Hebrews 10:15-18

Under the old covenant it was all about you- <u>thou shall do </u>but under the new, it is all about the Father and His- I WILL!

The Old Covenant provided animal sacrifices that served as an annual reminder of sins and led to death. Christ's death ushered in the New Covenant. He died in our place to take God's punishment for our sins. As a result, God remembers our sins no more. The sin issue has been settled with God. No other sacrifice is required to gain more forgiveness. We have everything we need under this new covenant. Jesus Christ has done it all.

The new covenant is not lawless. We have the Law of Christ (1 Corinthians 9:21) the Royal law of Love (James 2:8) the perfect law of liberty (James 1:25) the Law of Faith (Romans 3:27) These commandments we have are (see John 15:12) to believe in the name of his Son, Jesus Christ, and to love one another as he commanded us. (1 John 3:23).

God said: "Their sins and their lawless deeds I will remember no more". (See Hebrews 10:17)

In the New Testament we approach God in a: "New and Living Way", not in fear or with a conscience of sin. (See Hebrews 10:20 and 10:22)

In the New Testament we worship God in: "Spirit and truth", not in works and/or ceremony. (See John 4:24)

<u>The old is about do, do and do more. The new is about it is done!</u>

NOTES

WEEK SEVEN
Entering God's Rest

With billions spend on getaways, holidays, and spa`s we can see that mankind seek a rest not achievable through natural means. The vast majority come back needing a holiday from their holiday. True rest is found in a person. The promised sabbath rest spoken in scripture is found not in observations to keeping the requirements of sabbath keeping. According to the Jewish faith to keep the Sabbath holy, Jews were not supposed to work on Saturdays. To clarify this, Rabbis created 39 separate categories of what "work" means, and within those 39 categories there are many sub-categories. So, to follow the rule of not working on the Sabbath, there are literally thousands of sub-rules to follow, including how many steps you can take (no more than 2000 steps for the day), and how many letters you can write on the Sabbath for instance.

In the book of Hebrews which is written primarily to the Jews the anonymous author reminds us that there remains, then a Sabbath-rest for the people of God; for anyone who enters God's rest also rests from his own work, just as God did from His. Hebrews 4:9-10

The Sabbath is not and has never been Sunday.

The Sabbath was first mentioned in Scripture in Exodus 16, when the Lord started miraculously providing the children of Israel with manna in the wilderness. Shortly after this, the Lord commanded the observance of the Sabbath day in the ten commandments a sign that was communicated to Moses on Mt. Sinai on the two tablets of stone (Ex. 20:8-11 Remember the Sabbath day by keeping it holy. 9 Six days you shall labor and do all your work, 10 but the seventh day is a sabbath to the Lord your God. On it you shall not do any work, neither you, nor your son or daughter, nor your male or female servant, nor your animals, nor any foreigner residing in your towns. 11 For in six days the Lord made the heavens and the earth, the sea, and all that is in them, but he rested on the seventh day. Therefore, the Lord blessed the Sabbath day and made it holy.). In this command, God connected this Sabbath day with the rest that He took on the seventh day of creation. This rest was not because God was tired but because He was finished. Think of it this way, just as a painter completes his masterpiece knowing that adding even one more brush stroke will ruin his masterpiece, so to was it with God. His creation was prefect, so He rested.

Man was created on the sixth day, one day before the day of rest. Man was born into rest.

Deuteronomy 5:15, also clearly states that the Sabbath was to serve as a reminder to the Jews that they had been slaves in Egypt and were delivered from bondage, not by their own efforts, but by the supernatural power of God.

The sabbath day was given exclusively to the nation of Israel and never to any gentiles. Also no one before the giving of the Ten Commandments ever kept a sabbath day. In the New Testament, there is an even clearer purpose of the Sabbath stated.

In Colossians 2:16-17, Paul the Apostle reveals that the Sabbath was only a shadow of things to come and is now fulfilled in Christ. Hebrews 4:1-11 We may fear, then, lest a promise being left of entering into His rest, any one of you may seem to have come short, 2 for we also are having good news proclaimed, even as they, but the word heard did not profit them, not being mixed with faith in those who heard, 3 for we do enter into the rest—we who did believe, as He said, 'So I sware in My anger, If they shall enter into My rest—;' and yet the works were done from the foundation of the world, 4 for He spake in a certain place concerning the seventh [day] thus: 'And God did rest in the seventh day from all His works;' 5 and in this [place] again, 'If they shall enter into My rest—;' 6 since then, it remaineth for certain to enter into it, <u>and those who did first hear good news entered not in because of unbelief</u>—7 again He doth limit a certain day, 'To-day,' (in David saying, after so long a time,) as it hath been said, 'To-day, if His voice ye may hear, ye may not harden your hearts,' 8 for if Joshua had given them rest, He would not concerning another day have spoken after these things; 9 there doth remain, then, a sabbatic rest to the people of God, 10 for he who did enter into his rest, he also rested from his works, as God from His own.

11 May we be diligent, then, to enter into that rest, that no one in the same example of the <u>unbelief</u> may fall" talks about a Sabbath rest that is available to, but not necessarily functional in, all New Testament believers.

This New Testament Sabbath rest is simply a relationship with God in which we have ceased from doing things by our own efforts and are letting God work through us (Gal. 2:20 I have been crucified with Christ; and it is no longer I who live, but Christ lives in me; and the life which I now live in the flesh I live by faith in the Son of God, who loved me and gave Himself up for me; Heb. 4:10 For the one who has entered His rest has himself also rested from his works, as God did from His.). The Sabbath is not a day, but rather a relationship with God through Jesus. Rest in His love and let Him use you today.

Jesus said: "...the Son of Man is also Lord of the Sabbath." (Mark 2:28)

This rest or relationship refers to an inner posture of trust and quiet confidence in Jesus' finished work and in His ability to give you increase and good success as you go about doing what you need to do. Rest is not sitting around doing nothing and waiting for His blessings to fall into our laps.

Beloved, what God doesn't want you to do is worry and do things out of fear, guilt, or judgement. He wants you to rest at Jesus' feet and listen to His words of love and life. Let His love drive out your fears!

It is finished! Rest!

We are complete in Christ Jesus alone and fully restored in our relationship with "Abba" Father.

God has provided a permanent rest for us through the New Covenant. Our promised land is in our relationship with Jesus Christ. Everything is provided in Him. He offers a life of love, joy, and peace to all who would receive it. That even in a season of presser we can be at rest in Him. Jesus is our Sabbath rest!

The only way to enter this rest is by faith. In order to rest, we must stop striving. It is impossible to experience the abundant life in Christ while we are still trying to make ourselves acceptable before God by our own works. We must believe and trust in what Christ has done for us at the cross. Just as one's father makes provisions in his last will for your inheritance, God has made us holy and acceptable in His sight through the New Covenant. Making us co-heirs with Christ Jesus.

Therefore, brothers, since we have confidence to enter the Most Holy Place by the Blood of Jesus, by a new and living way opened for us through the curtain, that is, his Body, and since we have a great priest over the house of God, let us draw near to God with a sincere heart in full assurance of faith, having our hearts sprinkled to cleanse us from a guilty conscience and having our bodies washed with pure water. Let us hold unswervingly to the hope we profess, for he who promised is faithful. Hebrews 10:19-23

Are you still trying to live the Christian life in your own strength under law?

Write down a few areas where you are performing to get the fathers approval?

God has provided a new and living way whereby we can enter into a permanent Sabbath Rest. Are you willing to enter in by faith today? Write down some steps you think you can take to enter into His permanent sabbath rest?

How do we labor to enter his rest?

The work we rest from is the dead work of trying to earn God's favour and approval.

There remains, then, a Sabbath-rest for the people of God; for anyone who enters God's rest also rests from his own work, just as God did from his. Let us, therefore, make every effort to enter that rest, so that no one will fall by following their example of unbelief (some translation say disobedience, but it is more accurately translated unbelief. (Heb 4:9-11 Youngs literal translation reads there doth remain, then, a sabbatic rest to the people of God, 10 for he who did enter into his rest, he also rested from his works, as God from His own. 11 May we be diligent, then, to enter into that rest, that no one in the same example of the unbelief may fall,).

Read the passage in context and you will see that it is referring to the unbelieving children of Israel. They tried to earn what God wanted to give them and consequently they never entered the Lord's rest.

If you don't believe that God wants to bless you and, indeed, that he already has blessed you with every blessing in Christ Jesus, then you will work and never rest. You will exhaust yourself trying to get what he has already given.

You may work for salvation, sanctification, and even a reward, but if you are trying instead of trusting you will be anxious and insecure. You will always wonder, have I done enough?

Some might say it was because "They didn't keep God's law. You've got to strive and work to keep the commands." Under old the law-keeping covenant this was absolutely true, but in the new covenant the only real work is that which flows out of faith in Jesus Christ (John 6:29 Jesus answered and said to them, 'This is the work of God, that ye may believe in him whom He did send.').

The issue is not what you do but what you believe, because what you do follows what you believe. Disobedience is a fruit not a root. The Israelites' problem was not that they broke the rules but that they distrusted God:

For we also have had the gospel preached to us, just as they did; but the message they heard was of no value to them, because those who heard did not combine it with faith. (Heb 4:2)

Faith does not compel God to forgive us or sanctify us. Faith doesn't make God do anything. Rather, faith is a positive response to what God has done. Faith is acknowledging every good thing that is already ours in Christ (2 Pet 1:3 seeing that His divine power has granted to us everything pertaining to life and godliness, through the true knowledge of Him who called us by His own glory and excellence).

Faith doesn't make things real that weren't real to begin with, but faith makes them real to you. For instance, if you battle with guilt and condemnation, you don't need Jesus to come and take away your sin.

You need to believe he already did. Jesus is the cure for guilt, but until you believe it, you won't be cured.

Faith is not a work; faith is a rest. Faith is a noun, not a verb. Faith is a persuasion that God is who he says he is, has done what he said he's done, and will do what he has promised to do. Consider Abraham, who...

...did not waver through unbelief regarding the promise of God, but was strengthened in his faith and gave glory to God, being fully persuaded that God had power to do what he had promised. (Rom 4:20-21)

Faith is being fully persuaded. When you are fully persuaded, you can rest. The issue is settled. Your mind is made up and your heart is at ease.

The promises of God are Yes and Amen! (see 2 Corinthians 1:20)

If you do not trust God to take care of you and provide for your needs, you will work. Far better to labour towards a place of trust where you cease from your dead works and allow your heart to be established in true righteousness bear fruit. Do you see? You don't work to earn rest but to enter his rest. Big difference.

Historical evidence that the sabbath day given to the Jew was never given to the Church.

There is zero historical fact that Christian kept a sabbath day. Rather there is overwhelming evidence of Believers keeping the first day of the week.

What we call Sunday. The Apostles in 33 AD were already worshiping on the first day of the week. (Sunday). Why because it was the day the Lord was raised. Unlike the sabbath of the old covenant which was a sign for the Jews. Sunday is not a sign of the new covenant to Christians. Those signs are communion, and water baptism which was previously explained.

Acts 20:7 On the first day of the week, we gathered with the local believers to share in the Lord's Supper. Paul was preaching to them, and since he was leaving the next day, he kept talking until...

1 Cor 16:1-2 Now about the collection for the Lord's people: Do what I told the Galatian churches to do. 2 On the first day of every week, each one of you should set aside a sum of money in keeping with your income, saving it up, so that when I come no collections will have to be made.

150AD JUSTIN: Moreover, all those righteous men already mentioned [after mentioning Adam. Abel, Enoch, Lot, Noah, Melchizedek, and Abraham], though they kept no Sabbaths, were pleasing to God; and after them Abraham with all his descendants until Moses... And you [fleshly Jews] were commanded to keep Sabbaths, that you might retain the memorial of God. For His word makes this announcement, saying, "That you may know that I am God who redeemed you." (Dialogue With Trypho the Jew, 150-165 AD, Ante-Nicene Fathers, vol. 1, page 204)

200AD TERTULLIAN: Let him who contends that the Sabbath is still to be observed a balm of salvation, and circumcision on the eighth day because of threat of death, teach us that in earliest times righteous men kept Sabbath or practiced circumcision, and so were made friends of God. ...Therefore, since God originated Adam uncircumcised, and inobservant of the Sabbath, consequently his offspring also, Abel, offering Him sacrifices, uncircumcised and inobservant of the Sabbath, was by Him commended... Noah also, uncircumcised - yes, and inobservant of the Sabbath - God freed from the deluge. For Enoch, too, most righteous man, uncircumcised and inobservant of the Sabbath, He translated from this world... Melchizedek also, "the priest of most high God," uncircumcised and inobservant of the Sabbath, was chosen to the priesthood of God. (An Answer to the Jews 2:10; 4:1, Ante-Nicene Fathers Vol. 3, page 153)

220 AD Origen "Hence it is not possible that the [day of] rest after the Sabbath should have come into existence from the seventh [day] of our God. On the contrary, it is our Savior who, after the pattern of his own rest, caused us to be made in the likeness of his death, and hence also of his resurrection" (Commentary on John 2:28).

225 AD The Didascalia "The apostles further appointed: On the first day of the week let there be service, and the reading of the Holy Scriptures, and the oblation, because on the first day of the week our Lord rose from the place of the dead, and on the first day of the week he arose upon the world, and on the first day of the week he ascended up to heaven, and on the first day of the week he will appear at last with the angels of heaven" (Didascalia 2).

250AD CYPRIAN: The eight day, that is, the first day after the Sabbath, and the Lord's Day." (Epistle 58, Sec 4)

The first historical record of methodical Sabbath Keeping by Christians who stopped worshipping on the first day of the week, was two active Anabaptist leaders, Andreas Fisher, and Oswald Glait, became the pioneer and promoters of the Sabbath for Christians in 1527 AD.

Rest is not activity or lack of activity, but the present and abiding peace of God.

BUT WHAT ABOUT DOING the work of God? Let's expand:

Then they asked him, "What shall we do that we may work the works of God?" What did Jesus tell them to do? Did he tell them to go and feed the hungry, to clothe the naked, to visit the widow and the fatherless in their affliction? Perhaps you may say that, according to scripture, is "pure and undefiled religion." Granted; but something comes before that. That is all right and necessary in its place. But when these men wanted to know what they had to do to inherit eternal life, Jesus said: "This is the work of God, that ye believe on him whom he hath sent."

DL Moody (1891), *Sovereign Grace*

EscapeToReality.org

JOHN 6:28-29 THEN THEY said to Him, "What shall we do, that we may work the works of God?" Jesus answered and said to them, "This is the work of God, that you believe in Him whom He sent."

When you have seen the beauty of Jesus, faith comes easily. Unbelief is the harder choice. To fold your arms and lock your jaw as the goodness of God assails you from every direction requires real commitment.

Unbelief is not passive ignorance. Unbelief is hardening your heart to the manifest goodness of God. Unbelief is cursing that which God has blessed and hating that which he loves. Unbelief is resisting the Holy Spirit and clinging to worthless idols (Acts 7:51 You men who are stiff-necked and uncircumcised in heart and ears are always resisting the Holy Spirit; you are doing just as your fathers did, Acts 14:15 and saying, "Men, why are you doing these things? We are also men of the same nature as you and preach the gospel to you that you should turn from these [a]vain things to a living God, who made the heaven and the earth and the sea and all that is in them, Acts 19:9 Also, many of those who had practiced magic brought their books together and burned them in the sight of all. And they counted up the value of them, and it totaled fifty thousand pieces of silver.).

I am not talking about people who haven't heard the gospel. I'm talking about those who encountered the love and grace of God and have rejected it. Instead of opening the door to the One who knocks (easy), they've locked it.

Look at how unbelief is described in the New Testament, and you will find plenty of verbs or action words. Unbelief is *rejecting* Jesus (John 3:36) and *denying* the Lord (see ref. Jude 1:4). It's *thrusting away* the word of God and *judging* yourself unworthy of life (see ref Acts 13:46). It's *suppressing* the truth (see ref. Rom 1:18) and *delighting* in wickedness (see ref. 2 Th 2:12). It's *turning away* (see ref. Heb 12:25), *going astray* (see ref. 2 Pet 2:15), and *trampling* the Son of God underfoot (see ref. Heb 10:29).

And how does Jesus describe unbelievers? As evil*doers* and *workers* of iniquity (see ref. Matt 7:23).

<u>Do you see?</u> It takes hard work to succeed as an unbeliever. You need to apply yourself with religious dedication. It's a life-time commitment with no days off. You cannot afford to drop your guard even for a moment or Jesus might sneak up and hug you. <u>If faith is a rest, unbelief is restlessness:</u>

And to whom sware he that they should not enter into his rest, but to them that believed not? So, we see that they could not enter in because of unbelief. (Heb 3:18-19, KJV)

NOTES

WEEK EIGHT
Church

The Greek word for "church" is ecclesia and literally means an assembly of people together for the purpose of worship or prayer or praise or just looking unto God.

I'm going to add some other things here. It says, "Ecclesia in the New Testament can encompass any number of believers. It can be used of small groups that met in homes (Romans 16:5). It encompassed all believers living in a large city (Acts 11:22), or a large geographical district, such as Asia or Galatia." It goes on to say, "The typical meeting of the church was in a home. When such a congregation met 'everyone [had] a hymn, a word of instruction, a revelation, a tongue or an interpretation' (1 Corinthians 14:26). Individuals shared and others 'weighed carefully what was said' (1 Corinthians 14:29) ...such sharing remains essential to the very existence of the church as a community of faith...Each person was expected to contribute and to serve others with his or her spiritual gift(s)."

Chances are, you've heard someone say, "I love God, but I don't have to go to church to prove it." They're right! Jesus does not say, "And this is how you know that you love me—if you attend church." We saints are the Church.

If going to church is not required to show our love for God, what is the point of church?

The answer may surprise you. Part of your growth in Christ only happens when being in community with other believers. It is the equivalent of trying to become a great soccer player alone. There is only so much you can learn on your own; after a while you need to be on a team to really understand the sport and hone your skills.

Christianity is a team sport. We can definitely learn truths alone; however, these truths are fleshed out in community with other believers. As you learned on week four, part of being a disciple is uniting with other believers. If you want to be all God created you to be, it happens in biblical community.

Attending Weekly worship services contribute to our growth in multiple ways.

1. **It's a place to connect with other believers. (fellowship)**

"All...who had believed were together and had all things in common; and they began selling their property and possessions and were sharing them with all, as anyone might have need. Day by day continuing with one mind in the temple, breaking bread from house to house, they were taking their meals together with gladness and sincerity of heart..." (Acts 2:44–46)

Why should I attend church?

2. **It's a place to worship God.**

"Praise the Lord! Praise God in his sanctuary; praise him in his mighty heaven!" (Psalm 150:1)

We come to worship the ONE, the great I AM. Yes, we do this at home, in the car anywhere but there is something for collective praise and worship of our God, Lord and King.

3. **It's a place to hear Scripture taught.**

"All the believers devoted themselves to the apostles' teaching..." (Acts 2:42).

Where we can receive revelation from God. Have you possibly been in a service with a partner and you both received got two different messaged from the sermon.

It's because God spoke directly to what you need.

4. **It's a place to serve others.**

"God has given each of you a gift from his great variety of spiritual gifts. Use them well to serve one another" (1 Peter 4:10).

5. **It's a place to find encouragement.**

"And let us not neglect our meeting together, as some people do, but encourage one another, especially now that the day of his return is drawing near" (Hebrews 10:25).

6. **It's a place to be challenged.**

"As iron sharpens iron, so one man sharpens another" (Proverbs 27:17).

The Relationship

In Ephesians 4, Paul shares how each person in the body of Christ is important and needed. "As each part does its own special work, it helps the other parts grow, so that the whole body is healthy and growing and full of love" (Ephesians 4:16 NLT). Each Christian has something to contribute to the church. When we are willing to get involved, serve, and work together— "the whole body is healthy and growing and full of love."

When speaking to believers in Corinth, Paul tells them that they are dependent upon each other. "The way God designed our bodies is a model for understanding our lives together as a church: every part dependent on every other part" (1 Corinthians 12:25). It's not only nice to be with other believers; it's necessary. We need each other.

Part of our growth in Christ only happens when being in community with other believers. The Key is that we live from His life.

How do you find a group of believers that's right for you?

• Pray for discernment and leading.

• Look for a church that faithfully teaches God's Word, Grace and not a mixture of covenants.

• Find a church that is full of love and full of the Holy Spirit. Flowing in the gifts of the Holy Spirit such as prophecy and healing.

• Find a church that is serious about revealing your new identity as sons and daughters of God (Grace based disciples).

• Get involved.

• If it fits—stay; if it doesn't fit—find a church that does.

Take ownership not membership.

Church is not a spectator sport!

NOTES

CONCLUSION

Congratulations! You have reached the end of this 8 weeks. Now what?

For those interested look out for the 12-week foundations course. A more in-depth with additional topics such as Repentance and Discipleship.

ABOUT THE AUTHOR

P aul de Sousa is a Is a son of God. Teacher and A serial entrepreneur. Paul shares his thoughts and insights on several social media platforms reaching tens of thousands weekly.

His Material has reached over 1 million monthly via email. Thanks to the generous donations of believers.

His first book in the Entrepreneurs space is The Entrepreneurs Blueprint: Think it, Fund it, Built it, Sell it!

Available at Amazon, Apple, Kobo, Barnes and Noble and all other good bookstores.

COURSE SUMMARY

WEEK ONE – **I am found in Christ and Christ in me. I am Made NEW: this is to say** <u>You are not improved, re-modified, re-tweaked, re-conditioned, re-upholstered, re-vamped or re-branded.</u> **You are wholly new.**

WEEK TWO - The real purpose of salvation is to have intimacy—a personal relationship with the Lord God. Part of Salvation in essence was to get Heaven into You.

WEEK THREE - life begins through Christ the source of LIFE. Eternal life that produces everlasting life doesn't start when some trumpet blows, and Jesus comes or when you get to heaven one day. It starts the very moment you get born again

WEEK FOUR- The Bible is God's revelation of Himself, His LOVE letter and plan for redemption for all of humanity. Religions consists of man's thoughts about God, but the Bible isn't a compilation of men's thoughts—it contains God's thoughts.

WEEK FIVE - Water Baptism is an act that expresses one's faith in Jesus. Without that faith, the act means nothing. Water baptism doesn't wash away sins; it is only the blood of Jesus that has. But faith applies His blood to you.

There is a difference between being born again and the baptism of the Holy Spirit. At the new birth our nature changes. At the baptism in the Holy Spirit our ability changes!

WEEK SIX - God Himself looks at the cross as the dividing line of redemptions plan and the new way He has choose to deal with all mankind. A covenant is the same word for a testament, agreement or will. For a will or covenant to go into effect, the one who made it must die. Most of us understand this from our legal systems. If you have a will, it will not go into effect until you die.

The Law is Holy but when it flows through man's sinful flesh, it shows just how utterly sinful we truly are. The Law is holy, but it cannot make us holy. The Law reveals who we are, but it cannot remove our blemishes.

The Old Covenant provided animal sacrifices that served as an annual reminder of sins and led to death. Christ's death ushered in the New Covenant. He died in our place to take God's punishment for our sins. As a result, God remembers our sins no more. The sin issue has been settled with God. No other sacrifice is required to gain more forgiveness.

WEEK SEVEN – The New Testament Sabbath rest is simply a relationship with God in which we have ceased from doing things by our own efforts and are letting God work through us (Gal. 2:20 I have been crucified with Christ; and it is no longer I who live, but Christ lives in me; and the life which I now live in the flesh I live by faith in the Son of God, who loved me and gave Himself up for me; Heb. 4:10 For the one who has entered His rest has himself also rested from his works, as God did from His.). The Sabbath is not a day, but rather a relationship with God through Jesus. Rest in His love and let Him use you today.

WEEK EIGHT - Part of your growth in Christ only happens when being in community with other believers. There is only so much you can learn on your own.

Don't miss out!

Visit the website below and you can sign up to receive emails whenever Paul de Sousa publishes a new book. There's no charge and no obligation.

https://books2read.com/r/B-A-XBRV-DDUDC

BOOKS 2 READ

Connecting independent readers to independent writers.

Did you love *Foundations 8-Week Bible Course*? Then you should read *Entrepreneurs Blueprint*[1] by Paul de Sousa!

WARNING: The contents of this book can dramatically help you start your business, grow your sales, create enduring scale, and change your life forever. If you want <u>serious results</u>, and are sick and tired of trying, and banging your head on an immovable wall, then this book is a must read.

Learn the pro-tips, strategies, tactics, and resources of the incredibly successful entrepreneurs, founders, innovators, managers, and business on the planet for faster and more reliable revenue to help you realize *undreamed-of success*!With resources like a 10 000 investors and funders detailed database, free accounting software, a list of ninety plus free template and so much more within the <u>resource took kit</u>.These pro-tips,

---

1. https://books2read.com/u/bOnqd9

2. https://books2read.com/u/bOnqd9

strategies, tactics and resources, and a clear blueprint to how to Think it, Built it, Fund it, and Sell it!Here's a little of what you'll learn:

Learn the how to and vital importance of canvas modelling your idea.Learn how to sell more and drive more hot traffic through not only normal channels like Facebook, but even more effective alternatives.Learn how to build a loyal fan base for your brand that can generate epic sales.How to build a highly scale-able business with access to financial and distribution resourcesLearn the basics of financials and get a list of key financial numbers you got to know if you want to grow, scale and exitCritical sales tools for ecommerce and brick and mortar to a possible 8 figure revenueand so much more.

In this book there are summary stories from top entrepreneurs, founders, and start-ups who had major breakouts.

So, if you're a serious entrepreneur who wants the right tools to take it to the next level then the *Entrepreneur's Blueprint* is a must have essential resource tool!